Football Stadium

Bucket List Journal

The Publisher: Wandering Walks of Wonder Publishing

Kansas City, MO 64118

USA

Website: www.wanderingwalksofwonder.com

ISBN-13: 978-1517388102

ISBN-10: 1517388104

This exploration journal is a way to track your progress as you visit all the major league and college stadiums across the US and Canada.

There currently are 32 National Football League Stadium and countless College and High School Stadiums across the United States.

Going to a National Football League or College Game is one of America's favorite pastime and the easiest sport to get to check off those most wanted stadiums on your bucket list.

Stadium Location Map

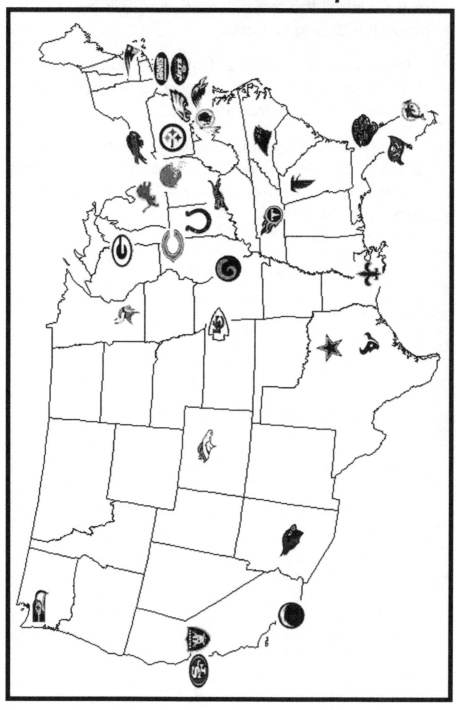

Stadium Name:	Date:
City/State:	
Home Team Name:	Visiting Team Name:

Weather:

Temperature:_____

Seat Number and Location

_____

	Q1	Q2	Q3	Q4	Final
Visitors					
Home					

Winning Quarterback_____   Losing Quarterback_____

Stadium Description

_____

_____

_____

_____

_____

_____

What did you enjoy most about the stadium?

_____
_____
_____
_____
_____
_____

What was the most memorable part of the game?

_____
_____
_____
_____
_____
_____

Did the stadium have a signature food or drink? How was it?

_____
_____
_____
_____
_____
_____

How were the fans?

_____

_____

_____

_____

_____

How was the in-game entertainment?
(Announcer, Music, mascots, fun events)

_____

_____

_____

_____

_____

What other sites did you see in the city during
your visit?

_____

_____

_____

_____

_____

Record other thoughts about the stadium or
tape your game ticket here.

_____

_____

_____

_____

_____

_____

_____

_____

_____

_____

_____

_____

_____

_____

_____

_____

_____

_____

_____

Stadium Name:	Date:
City/State:	

Home Team Name:	Visiting Team Name:

Weather:	Seat Number and Location
	_____
Temperature:_____	

	Q1	Q2	Q3	Q4	Final
Visitors					
Home					

Winning Quarterback_____   Losing Quarterback_____

Stadium Description

_____

_____

_____

_____

_____

_____

What did you enjoy most about the stadium?

_____
_____
_____
_____
_____

What was the most memorable part of the game?

_____
_____
_____
_____
_____

Did the stadium have a signature food or drink? How was it?

_____
_____
_____
_____
_____

How were the fans?

_____

_____

_____

_____

_____

_____

How was the in-game entertainment?
(Announcer, Music, mascots, fun events)

_____

_____

_____

_____

_____

_____

What other sites did you see in the city during
your visit?

_____

_____

_____

_____

_____

_____

Record other thoughts about the stadium or
tape your game ticket here.

_____

_____

_____

_____

_____

_____

_____

_____

_____

_____

_____

_____

_____

_____

_____

_____

_____

_____

_____

Stadium Name:	Date:

City/State:

Home Team Name:	Visiting Team Name:

Weather:	Seat Number and Location

Temperature:_____

	Q1	Q2	Q3	Q4		Final
Visitors						
Home						

Winning Quarterback_____   Losing Quarterback_____

Stadium Description

_____

_____

_____

_____

_____

_____

What did you enjoy most about the stadium?

_____

_____

_____

_____

_____

_____

What was the most memorable part of the game?

_____

_____

_____

_____

_____

Did the stadium have a signature food or drink? How was it?

_____

_____

_____

_____

_____

_____

How were the fans?

_____

_____

_____

_____

_____

How was the in-game entertainment?
(Announcer, Music, mascots, fun events)

_____

_____

_____

_____

_____

What other sites did you see in the city during
your visit?

_____

_____

_____

_____

_____

Record other thoughts about the stadium or
tape your game ticket here.

Stadium Name:	Date:

City/State:

Home Team Name:	Visiting Team Name:

Weather:	Seat Number and Location
	_____
Temperature:_____	

	Q1	Q2	Q3	Q4	Final
Visitors					
Home					

Winning Quarterback_____   Losing Quarterback_____

Stadium Description

_____

_____

_____

_____

_____

_____

What did you enjoy most about the stadium?

_____

_____

_____

_____

_____

What was the most memorable part of the game?

_____

_____

_____

_____

_____

Did the stadium have a signature food or drink? How was it?

_____

_____

_____

_____

_____

How were the fans?

_____

_____

_____

_____

_____

_____

How was the in-game entertainment?
(Announcer, Music, mascots, fun events)

_____

_____

_____

_____

_____

_____

What other sites did you see in the city during
your visit?

_____

_____

_____

_____

_____

_____

Record other thoughts about the stadium or tape your game ticket here.

_____

_____

_____

_____

_____

_____

_____

_____

_____

_____

_____

_____

_____

_____

_____

_____

_____

_____

Stadium Name:	Date:
City/State:	
Home Team Name:	Visiting Team Name:

Weather:

Temperature:_____

Seat Number and Location

	Q1	Q2	Q3	Q4	Final
Visitors					
Home					

Winning Quarterback_____   Losing Quarterback_____

Stadium Description

_____

_____

_____

_____

_____

_____

What did you enjoy most about the stadium?

_____
_____
_____
_____
_____

What was the most memorable part of the game?

_____
_____
_____
_____
_____

Did the stadium have a signature food or drink? How was it?

_____
_____
_____
_____
_____

How were the fans?

_____

_____

_____

_____

_____

_____

How was the in-game entertainment?
(Announcer, Music, mascots, fun events)

_____

_____

_____

_____

_____

What other sites did you see in the city during
your visit?

_____

_____

_____

_____

_____

Record other thoughts about the stadium or tape your game ticket here.

_____

_____

_____

_____

_____

_____

_____

_____

_____

_____

_____

_____

_____

_____

_____

_____

_____

_____

_____

_____

Stadium Name:	Date:
City/State:	
Home Team Name:	Visiting Team Name:

Weather:

Temperature:_____

Seat Number and Location

_____

	Q1	Q2	Q3	Q4	Final
Visitors					
Home					

Winning Quarterback_____   Losing Quarterback_____

Stadium Description

_____

_____

_____

_____

_____

_____

What did you enjoy most about the stadium?

_____

_____

_____

_____

_____

What was the most memorable part of the game?

_____

_____

_____

_____

_____

Did the stadium have a signature food or drink? How was it?

_____

_____

_____

_____

_____

How were the fans?

_____

_____

_____

_____

_____

How was the in-game entertainment?
(Announcer, Music, mascots, fun events)

_____

_____

_____

_____

_____

What other sites did you see in the city during
your visit?

_____

_____

_____

_____

_____

Record other thoughts about the stadium or
tape your game ticket here.

Stadium Name:	Date:
City/State:	

Home Team Name:	Visiting Team Name:

Weather:	Seat Number and Location
	_____
Temperature:_____	

	Q1	Q2	Q3	Q4	Final
Visitors					
Home					

Winning Quarterback_____   Losing Quarterback_____

Stadium Description

_____

_____

_____

_____

_____

_____

What did you enjoy most about the stadium?

_____

_____

_____

_____

_____

_____

What was the most memorable part of the game?

_____

_____

_____

_____

_____

Did the stadium have a signature food or drink? How was it?

_____

_____

_____

_____

_____

How were the fans?

_____

_____

_____

_____

_____

How was the in-game entertainment?
(Announcer, Music, mascots, fun events)

_____

_____

_____

_____

_____

What other sites did you see in the city during
your visit?

_____

_____

_____

_____

_____

Record other thoughts about the stadium or tape your game ticket here.

Stadium Name:	Date:
City/State:	
Home Team Name:	Visiting Team Name:

Weather:	Seat Number and Location
	_____
Temperature:_____	

	Q1	Q2	Q3	Q4	Final
Visitors					
Home					

Winning Quarterback_____   Losing Quarterback_____

Stadium Description

_____

_____

_____

_____

_____

_____

What did you enjoy most about the stadium?

_____

_____

_____

_____

_____

What was the most memorable part of the game?

_____

_____

_____

_____

_____

Did the stadium have a signature food or drink? How was it?

_____

_____

_____

_____

_____

How were the fans?

_____

_____

_____

_____

_____

_____

How was the in-game entertainment?
(Announcer, Music, mascots, fun events)

_____

_____

_____

_____

_____

_____

What other sites did you see in the city during
your visit?

_____

_____

_____

_____

_____

_____

Record other thoughts about the stadium or
tape your game ticket here.

Stadium Name:	Date:

City/State:

Home Team Name:	Visiting Team Name:

Weather:	Seat Number and Location

Temperature:_____

	Q1	Q2	Q3	Q4	Final
Visitors					
Home					

Winning Quarterback_____   Losing Quarterback_____

Stadium Description

_____

_____

_____

_____

_____

_____

What did you enjoy most about the stadium?

_____

_____

_____

_____

_____

What was the most memorable part of the game?

_____

_____

_____

_____

_____

Did the stadium have a signature food or drink? How was it?

_____

_____

_____

_____

_____

How were the fans?

_____

_____

_____

_____

_____

How was the in-game entertainment?
(Announcer, Music, mascots, fun events)

_____

_____

_____

_____

_____

What other sites did you see in the city during
your visit?

_____

_____

_____

_____

_____

Record other thoughts about the stadium or
tape your game ticket here.

_____

_____

_____

_____

_____

_____

_____

_____

_____

_____

_____

_____

_____

_____

_____

_____

_____

_____

_____

Stadium Name:	Date:
City/State:	

Home Team Name:	Visiting Team Name:

Weather:	Seat Number and Location
Temperature:_____	

	Q1	Q2	Q3	Q4		Final
Visitors						
Home						

Winning Quarterback_____   Losing Quarterback_____

Stadium Description

_____

_____

_____

_____

_____

_____

What did you enjoy most about the stadium?

_____

_____

_____

_____

_____

What was the most memorable part of the game?

_____

_____

_____

_____

_____

Did the stadium have a signature food or drink? How was it?

_____

_____

_____

_____

_____

How were the fans?

_____

_____

_____

_____

_____

_____

How was the in-game entertainment?
(Announcer, Music, mascots, fun events)

_____

_____

_____

_____

_____

_____

What other sites did you see in the city during
your visit?

_____

_____

_____

_____

_____

_____

Record other thoughts about the stadium or
tape your game ticket here.

_____

_____

_____

_____

_____

_____

_____

_____

_____

_____

_____

_____

_____

_____

_____

_____

_____

_____

Stadium Name:	Date:

City/State:

Home Team Name:	Visiting Team Name:

Weather:	Seat Number and Location
Temperature:_____	

	Q1	Q2	Q3	Q4	Final
Visitors					
Home					

Winning Quarterback_____   Losing Quarterback_____

Stadium Description

_____

_____

_____

_____

_____

_____

What did you enjoy most about the stadium?

_____

_____

_____

_____

_____

What was the most memorable part of the game?

_____

_____

_____

_____

_____

Did the stadium have a signature food or drink? How was it?

_____

_____

_____

_____

_____

How were the fans?

_____

_____

_____

_____

_____

How was the in-game entertainment?
(Announcer, Music, mascots, fun events)

_____

_____

_____

_____

_____

What other sites did you see in the city during
your visit?

_____

_____

_____

_____

_____

Record other thoughts about the stadium or tape your game ticket here.

_____

_____

_____

_____

_____

_____

_____

_____

_____

_____

_____

_____

_____

_____

_____

_____

_____

_____

_____

_____

Stadium Name:	Date:

City/State:

Home Team Name:	Visiting Team Name:

Weather:	Seat Number and Location
	_____
Temperature:_____	

	Q1	Q2	Q3	Q4	Final
Visitors					
Home					

Winning Quarterback_____   Losing Quarterback_____

Stadium Description

_____

_____

_____

_____

_____

_____

What did you enjoy most about the stadium?

_____

_____

_____

_____

_____

_____

What was the most memorable part of the game?

_____

_____

_____

_____

_____

Did the stadium have a signature food or drink? How was it?

_____

_____

_____

_____

_____

How were the fans?

_____

_____

_____

_____

_____

How was the in-game entertainment?
(Announcer, Music, mascots, fun events)

_____

_____

_____

_____

What other sites did you see in the city during
your visit?

_____

_____

_____

_____

_____

Record other thoughts about the stadium or tape your game ticket here.

Stadium Name:	Date:

City/State:

Home Team Name:	Visiting Team Name:

Weather:	Seat Number and Location
Temperature:_____	

	Q1	Q2	Q3	Q4		Final
Visitors						
Home						

Winning Quarterback_____   Losing Quarterback_____

Stadium Description

_____

_____

_____

_____

_____

_____

What did you enjoy most about the stadium?

_____

_____

_____

_____

_____

What was the most memorable part of the game?

_____

_____

_____

_____

_____

Did the stadium have a signature food or drink? How was it?

_____

_____

_____

_____

_____

How were the fans?

_____

_____

_____

_____

_____

_____

How was the in-game entertainment?
(Announcer, Music, mascots, fun events)

_____

_____

_____

_____

_____

_____

What other sites did you see in the city during
your visit?

_____

_____

_____

_____

_____

_____

Record other thoughts about the stadium or
tape your game ticket here.

_____

_____

_____

_____

_____

_____

_____

_____

_____

_____

_____

_____

_____

_____

_____

_____

_____

_____

_____

_____

Stadium Name:	Date:

City/State:

Home Team Name:	Visiting Team Name:

Weather:	Seat Number and Location
	_____
Temperature:_____	

	Q1	Q2	Q3	Q4	Final
Visitors					
Home					

Winning Quarterback_____   Losing Quarterback_____

Stadium Description

_____

_____

_____

_____

_____

_____

What did you enjoy most about the stadium?

_____

_____

_____

_____

_____

What was the most memorable part of the game?

_____

_____

_____

_____

_____

Did the stadium have a signature food or drink? How was it?

_____

_____

_____

_____

_____

How were the fans?

_____

_____

_____

_____

_____

How was the in-game entertainment?
(Announcer, Music, mascots, fun events)

_____

_____

_____

_____

_____

What other sites did you see in the city during
your visit?

_____

_____

_____

_____

_____

Record other thoughts about the stadium or
tape your game ticket here.

Stadium Name:	Date:

City/State:

Home Team Name:	Visiting Team Name:

Weather:	Seat Number and Location

Temperature:_____

	Q1	Q2	Q3	Q4	Final
Visitors					
Home					

Winning Quarterback_____   Losing Quarterback_____

Stadium Description

_____

_____

_____

_____

_____

_____

What did you enjoy most about the stadium?

_____

_____

_____

_____

_____

What was the most memorable part of the game?

_____

_____

_____

_____

_____

Did the stadium have a signature food or drink? How was it?

_____

_____

_____

_____

_____

How were the fans?

_____

_____

_____

_____

_____

_____

How was the in-game entertainment?
(Announcer, Music, mascots, fun events)

_____

_____

_____

_____

_____

_____

What other sites did you see in the city during
your visit?

_____

_____

_____

_____

_____

_____

Record other thoughts about the stadium or
tape your game ticket here.

Stadium Name:	Date:

City/State:

Home Team Name:	Visiting Team Name:

Weather:	Seat Number and Location

Temperature:_____

	Q1	Q2	Q3	Q4	Final
Visitors					
Home					

Winning Quarterback_____   Losing Quarterback_____

Stadium Description

_____

_____

_____

_____

_____

_____

What did you enjoy most about the stadium?

_____

_____

_____

_____

_____

What was the most memorable part of the game?

_____

_____

_____

_____

_____

Did the stadium have a signature food or drink? How was it?

_____

_____

_____

_____

_____

How were the fans?

_____

_____

_____

_____

_____

_____

How was the in-game entertainment?
(Announcer, Music, mascots, fun events)

_____

_____

_____

_____

_____

_____

What other sites did you see in the city during
your visit?

_____

_____

_____

_____

_____

_____

Record other thoughts about the stadium or
tape your game ticket here.

Stadium Name:	Date:
City/State:	
Home Team Name:	Visiting Team Name:
Weather: Temperature:_____	Seat Number and Location

	Q1	Q2	Q3	Q4	Final
Visitors					
Home					

Winning Quarterback_____   Losing Quarterback_____

Stadium Description

_____

_____

_____

_____

_____

_____

What did you enjoy most about the stadium?

_____

_____

_____

_____

_____

What was the most memorable part of the game?

_____

_____

_____

_____

_____

Did the stadium have a signature food or drink? How was it?

_____

_____

_____

_____

_____

How were the fans?

_____
_____
_____
_____
_____
_____

How was the in-game entertainment?
(Announcer, Music, mascots, fun events)

_____
_____
_____
_____
_____

What other sites did you see in the city during
your visit?

_____
_____
_____
_____
_____

Record other thoughts about the stadium or
tape your game ticket here.

Stadium Name:	Date:
City/State:	

Home Team Name:	Visiting Team Name:

Weather:	Seat Number and Location
	_____
Temperature:_____	

	Q1	Q2	Q3	Q4	Final
Visitors					
Home					

Winning Quarterback_____ Losing Quarterback_____

Stadium Description

_____

_____

_____

_____

_____

_____

What did you enjoy most about the stadium?

_____

_____

_____

_____

_____

What was the most memorable part of the game?

_____

_____

_____

_____

_____

Did the stadium have a signature food or drink? How was it?

_____

_____

_____

_____

_____

How were the fans?

_____

_____

_____

_____

_____

How was the in-game entertainment?
(Announcer, Music, mascots, fun events)

_____

_____

_____

_____

_____

What other sites did you see in the city during
your visit?

_____

_____

_____

_____

_____

Record other thoughts about the stadium or tape your game ticket here.

_____

_____

_____

_____

_____

_____

_____

_____

_____

_____

_____

_____

_____

_____

_____

_____

_____

_____

_____

Stadium Name:	Date:
City/State:	

Home Team Name:	Visiting Team Name:

Weather:	Seat Number and Location

Temperature:_____

	Q1	Q2	Q3	Q4	Final
Visitors					
Home					

Winning Quarterback_____   Losing Quarterback_____

Stadium Description

_____

_____

_____

_____

_____

_____

What did you enjoy most about the stadium?

_____
_____
_____
_____
_____

What was the most memorable part of the game?

_____
_____
_____
_____
_____

Did the stadium have a signature food or drink? How was it?

_____
_____
_____
_____
_____

How were the fans?

_____

_____

_____

_____

_____

_____

How was the in-game entertainment?
(Announcer, Music, mascots, fun events)

_____

_____

_____

_____

_____

What other sites did you see in the city during
your visit?

_____

_____

_____

_____

_____

Record other thoughts about the stadium or tape your game ticket here.

Stadium Name:	Date:

City/State:

Home Team Name:	Visiting Team Name:

Weather:	Seat Number and Location
Temperature:_____	

	Q1	Q2	Q3	Q4	Final
Visitors					
Home					

Winning Quarterback_____   Losing Quarterback_____

Stadium Description

_____

_____

_____

_____

_____

_____

What did you enjoy most about the stadium?

_____

_____

_____

_____

_____

What was the most memorable part of the game?

_____

_____

_____

_____

_____

Did the stadium have a signature food or drink? How was it?

_____

_____

_____

_____

_____

How were the fans?

_____

_____

_____

_____

_____

How was the in-game entertainment?
(Announcer, Music, mascots, fun events)

_____

_____

_____

_____

_____

What other sites did you see in the city during
your visit?

_____

_____

_____

_____

_____

Record other thoughts about the stadium or tape your game ticket here.

Stadium Name:	Date:
City/State:	

Home Team Name:	Visiting Team Name:

Weather:	Seat Number and Location

Temperature:_____

	Q1	Q2	Q3	Q4	Final
Visitors					
Home					

Winning Quarterback_____   Losing Quarterback_____

Stadium Description

_____

_____

_____

_____

_____

_____

What did you enjoy most about the stadium?

_____

_____

_____

_____

_____

_____

What was the most memorable part of the game?

_____

_____

_____

_____

_____

Did the stadium have a signature food or drink? How was it?

_____

_____

_____

_____

_____

How were the fans?

_____

_____

_____

_____

_____

How was the in-game entertainment?
(Announcer, Music, mascots, fun events)

_____

_____

_____

_____

_____

What other sites did you see in the city during
your visit?

_____

_____

_____

_____

_____

Record other thoughts about the stadium or tape your game ticket here.

Stadium Name:	Date:
City/State:	

Home Team Name:	Visiting Team Name:

Weather:	Seat Number and Location

Temperature:_____

	Q1	Q2	Q3	Q4	Final
Visitors					
Home					

Winning Quarterback_____   Losing Quarterback_____

Stadium Description

_____

_____

_____

_____

_____

_____

What did you enjoy most about the stadium?

_____

_____

_____

_____

_____

_____

What was the most memorable part of the game?

_____

_____

_____

_____

_____

_____

Did the stadium have a signature food or drink? How was it?

_____

_____

_____

_____

_____

_____

How were the fans?

_____

_____

_____

_____

_____

_____

How was the in-game entertainment?
(Announcer, Music, mascots, fun events)

_____

_____

_____

_____

_____

What other sites did you see in the city during
your visit?

_____

_____

_____

_____

_____

Record other thoughts about the stadium or
tape your game ticket here.

_____

_____

_____

_____

_____

_____

_____

_____

_____

_____

_____

_____

_____

_____

_____

_____

_____

_____

_____

_____

Stadium Name:	Date:

City/State:

Home Team Name:	Visiting Team Name:

Weather:	Seat Number and Location

Temperature:_____

	Q1	Q2	Q3	Q4	Final
Visitors					
Home					

Winning Quarterback_____   Losing Quarterback_____

Stadium Description

_____

_____

_____

_____

_____

_____

What did you enjoy most about the stadium?

_____

_____

_____

_____

_____

What was the most memorable part of the game?

_____

_____

_____

_____

_____

Did the stadium have a signature food or drink? How was it?

_____

_____

_____

_____

_____

How were the fans?

_____

_____

_____

_____

_____

How was the in-game entertainment?
(Announcer, Music, mascots, fun events)

_____

_____

_____

_____

_____

What other sites did you see in the city during
your visit?

_____

_____

_____

_____

_____

Record other thoughts about the stadium or tape your game ticket here.

_____

_____

_____

_____

_____

_____

_____

_____

_____

_____

_____

_____

_____

_____

_____

_____

_____

_____

_____

Stadium Name:	Date:
City/State:	
Home Team Name:	Visiting Team Name:
Weather:	Seat Number and Location

Temperature:_____

	Q1	Q2	Q3	Q4	Final
Visitors					
Home					

Winning Quarterback_____   Losing Quarterback_____

Stadium Description

_____

_____

_____

_____

_____

_____

What did you enjoy most about the stadium?

_____

_____

_____

_____

_____

_____

What was the most memorable part of the game?

_____

_____

_____

_____

_____

Did the stadium have a signature food or drink? How was it?

_____

_____

_____

_____

_____

How were the fans?

_____

_____

_____

_____

_____

How was the in-game entertainment?
(Announcer, Music, mascots, fun events)

_____

_____

_____

_____

_____

What other sites did you see in the city during
your visit?

_____

_____

_____

_____

_____

Record other thoughts about the stadium or
tape your game ticket here.

_____

_____

_____

_____

_____

_____

_____

_____

_____

_____

_____

_____

_____

_____

_____

_____

_____

_____

_____

_____

_____

_____

Stadium Name:	Date:

City/State:

Home Team Name:	Visiting Team Name:

Weather:	Seat Number and Location

Temperature:_____

	Q1	Q2	Q3	Q4	Final
Visitors					
Home					

Winning Quarterback_____   Losing Quarterback_____

Stadium Description

_____

_____

_____

_____

_____

_____

What did you enjoy most about the stadium?

_____

_____

_____

_____

_____

What was the most memorable part of the game?

_____

_____

_____

_____

_____

Did the stadium have a signature food or drink? How was it?

_____

_____

_____

_____

_____

How were the fans?

_____
_____
_____
_____
_____

How was the in-game entertainment?
(Announcer, Music, mascots, fun events)

_____
_____
_____
_____
_____

What other sites did you see in the city during
your visit?

_____
_____
_____
_____
_____

Record other thoughts about the stadium or
tape your game ticket here.

Stadium Name:	Date:
City/State:	
Home Team Name:	Visiting Team Name:

Weather:	Seat Number and Location

Temperature:_____

	Q1	Q2	Q3	Q4	Final
Visitors					
Home					

Winning Quarterback_____   Losing Quarterback_____

Stadium Description

_____

_____

_____

_____

_____

_____

What did you enjoy most about the stadium?

_____

_____

_____

_____

_____

What was the most memorable part of the game?

_____

_____

_____

_____

_____

Did the stadium have a signature food or drink? How was it?

_____

_____

_____

_____

_____

How were the fans?

_____

_____

_____

_____

_____

How was the in-game entertainment?
(Announcer, Music, mascots, fun events)

_____

_____

_____

_____

_____

What other sites did you see in the city during
your visit?

_____

_____

_____

_____

_____

Record other thoughts about the stadium or
tape your game ticket here.

Stadium Name:	Date:
City/State:	

Home Team Name:	Visiting Team Name:

Weather:	Seat Number and Location
Temperature:_____	

	Q1	Q2	Q3	Q4	Final
Visitors					
Home					

Winning Quarterback_____   Losing Quarterback_____

Stadium Description

_____
_____
_____
_____
_____
_____

What did you enjoy most about the stadium?

_____

_____

_____

_____

_____

_____

What was the most memorable part of the game?

_____

_____

_____

_____

_____

Did the stadium have a signature food or drink? How was it?

_____

_____

_____

_____

_____

How were the fans?

_____

_____

_____

_____

_____

How was the in-game entertainment?
(Announcer, Music, mascots, fun events)

_____

_____

_____

_____

_____

What other sites did you see in the city during
your visit?

_____

_____

_____

_____

_____

Record other thoughts about the stadium or tape your game ticket here.

_____

_____

_____

_____

_____

_____

_____

_____

_____

_____

_____

_____

_____

_____

_____

_____

_____

_____

_____

_____

Stadium Name:	Date:
City/State:	
Home Team Name:	Visiting Team Name:

Weather:

Temperature:_____

Seat Number and Location

	Q1	Q2	Q3	Q4	Final
Visitors					
Home					

Winning Quarterback_____   Losing Quarterback_____

Stadium Description

_____

_____

_____

_____

_____

_____

What did you enjoy most about the stadium?

_____

_____

_____

_____

_____

_____

What was the most memorable part of the game?

_____

_____

_____

_____

_____

_____

Did the stadium have a signature food or drink? How was it?

_____

_____

_____

_____

_____

_____

How were the fans?

_____

_____

_____

_____

_____

How was the in-game entertainment?
(Announcer, Music, mascots, fun events)

_____

_____

_____

_____

_____

What other sites did you see in the city during
your visit?

_____

_____

_____

_____

_____

Record other thoughts about the stadium or
tape your game ticket here.

Stadium Name:	Date:

City/State:

Home Team Name:	Visiting Team Name:

Weather:	Seat Number and Location
Temperature:_____	

	Q1	Q2	Q3	Q4		Final
Visitors						
Home						

Winning Quarterback_____   Losing Quarterback_____

Stadium Description

_____

_____

_____

_____

_____

_____

What did you enjoy most about the stadium?

_____

_____

_____

_____

_____

What was the most memorable part of the game?

_____

_____

_____

_____

_____

Did the stadium have a signature food or drink? How was it?

_____

_____

_____

_____

_____

How were the fans?

_____

_____

_____

_____

_____

How was the in-game entertainment?
(Announcer, Music, mascots, fun events)

_____

_____

_____

_____

_____

What other sites did you see in the city during
your visit?

_____

_____

_____

_____

_____

Record other thoughts about the stadium or
tape your game ticket here.

_____

_____

_____

_____

_____

_____

_____

_____

_____

_____

_____

_____

_____

_____

_____

_____

_____

_____

_____

_____

Stadium Name:	Date:
City/State:	
Home Team Name:	Visiting Team Name:
Weather:	Seat Number and Location

Temperature:_____

	Q1	Q2	Q3	Q4	Final
Visitors					
Home					

Winning Quarterback_____   Losing Quarterback_____

Stadium Description

_____

_____

_____

_____

_____

_____

What did you enjoy most about the stadium?

_____

_____

_____

_____

_____

_____

What was the most memorable part of the game?

_____

_____

_____

_____

_____

Did the stadium have a signature food or drink? How was it?

_____

_____

_____

_____

_____

How were the fans?

_____

_____

_____

_____

_____

How was the in-game entertainment?
(Announcer, Music, mascots, fun events)

_____

_____

_____

_____

_____

What other sites did you see in the city during
your visit?

_____

_____

_____

_____

_____

Record other thoughts about the stadium or
tape your game ticket here.

_____

_____

_____

_____

_____

_____

_____

_____

_____

_____

_____

_____

_____

_____

_____

_____

_____

Stadium Name:	Date:
City/State:	
Home Team Name:	Visiting Team Name:
Weather:	Seat Number and Location

Temperature:_____

	Q1	Q2	Q3	Q4	Final
Visitors					
Home					

Winning Quarterback_____   Losing Quarterback_____

Stadium Description

_____

_____

_____

_____

_____

_____

What did you enjoy most about the stadium?

_____
_____
_____
_____
_____

What was the most memorable part of the game?

_____
_____
_____
_____
_____

Did the stadium have a signature food or drink? How was it?

_____
_____
_____
_____
_____

How were the fans?

_____

_____

_____

_____

_____

_____

How was the in-game entertainment?
(Announcer, Music, mascots, fun events)

_____

_____

_____

_____

_____

_____

What other sites did you see in the city during
your visit?

_____

_____

_____

_____

_____

_____

Record other thoughts about the stadium or
tape your game ticket here.

Stadium Name:	Date:
City/State:	

Home Team Name:	Visiting Team Name:

Weather:	Seat Number and Location

Temperature:_____

	Q1	Q2	Q3	Q4	Final
Visitors					
Home					

Winning Quarterback_____   Losing Quarterback_____

Stadium Description

_____

_____

_____

_____

_____

_____

What did you enjoy most about the stadium?

_____

_____

_____

_____

_____

What was the most memorable part of the game?

_____

_____

_____

_____

_____

Did the stadium have a signature food or drink? How was it?

_____

_____

_____

_____

_____

_____

How were the fans?

_____

_____

_____

_____

_____

How was the in-game entertainment?
(Announcer, Music, mascots, fun events)

_____

_____

_____

_____

_____

What other sites did you see in the city during
your visit?

_____

_____

_____

_____

_____

Record other thoughts about the stadium or
tape your game ticket here.

_____

_____

_____

_____

_____

_____

_____

_____

_____

_____

_____

_____

_____

_____

_____

_____

_____

_____

Stadium Name:	Date:
City/State:	
Home Team Name:	Visiting Team Name:
Weather: Temperature:_____	Seat Number and Location _____

	Q1	Q2	Q3	Q4	Final
Visitors					
Home					

Winning Quarterback_____   Losing Quarterback_____

Stadium Description

_____

_____

_____

_____

_____

_____

What did you enjoy most about the stadium?

_____

_____

_____

_____

_____

_____

What was the most memorable part of the game?

_____

_____

_____

_____

_____

Did the stadium have a signature food or drink? How was it?

_____

_____

_____

_____

_____

How were the fans?

_____

_____

_____

_____

_____

_____

How was the in-game entertainment?
(Announcer, Music, mascots, fun events)

_____

_____

_____

_____

_____

What other sites did you see in the city during
your visit?

_____

_____

_____

_____

_____

Record other thoughts about the stadium or tape your game ticket here.

Stadium Name:	Date:

City/State:

Home Team Name:	Visiting Team Name:

Weather:	Seat Number and Location

Temperature:_____

	Q1	Q2	Q3	Q4	Final
Visitors					
Home					

Winning Quarterback_____   Losing Quarterback_____

Stadium Description

_____

_____

_____

_____

_____

_____

What did you enjoy most about the stadium?

_____

_____

_____

_____

_____

What was the most memorable part of the game?

_____

_____

_____

_____

_____

Did the stadium have a signature food or drink? How was it?

_____

_____

_____

_____

_____

How were the fans?

_____

_____

_____

_____

_____

How was the in-game entertainment?
(Announcer, Music, mascots, fun events)

_____

_____

_____

_____

_____

What other sites did you see in the city during
your visit?

_____

_____

_____

_____

_____

_____

Record other thoughts about the stadium or
tape your game ticket here.

_____

_____

_____

_____

_____

_____

_____

_____

_____

_____

_____

_____

_____

_____

_____

_____

_____

_____

Stadium Name:	Date:
City/State:	

Home Team Name:	Visiting Team Name:
Weather:	Seat Number and Location

Temperature:_____

	Q1	Q2	Q3	Q4	Final
Visitors					
Home					

Winning Quarterback_____   Losing Quarterback_____

Stadium Description

_____

_____

_____

_____

_____

_____

What did you enjoy most about the stadium?

_____

_____

_____

_____

_____

What was the most memorable part of the game?

_____

_____

_____

_____

_____

Did the stadium have a signature food or drink? How was it?

_____

_____

_____

_____

_____

How were the fans?

_____
_____
_____
_____
_____
_____

How was the in-game entertainment?
(Announcer, Music, mascots, fun events)

_____
_____
_____
_____
_____
_____

What other sites did you see in the city during
your visit?

_____
_____
_____
_____
_____
_____

Record other thoughts about the stadium or
tape your game ticket here.

If you enjoyed this journal, we have many more styles and types to choose from. Visit our website for a complete list of journals.

www.wanderingwalksofwonder.com

Baseball Stadiums Journal

Bucket List Journal

National Parks Journal

Lighthouse Exploration Journal

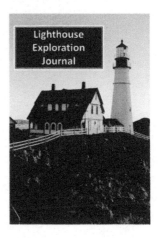